"Dr. Castellanos presents a refreshingly integrated ... sexual health that includes the physical and psychological dimensions. This book offers you a clear and concise roadmap to identify your stumbling blocks to good sex and sexual pleasure, and then to move beyond them."
- **Esther Perel, author of *Mating in Captivity***

"A wonderful guide for anyone looking for helpful, compassionate advice on regaining sexual desire and having a more satisfying sex life."
- **Debby Herbenick, PhD, Associate Professor at Indiana University and author of *Sex Made Easy***

"Wanting To Want is truly revolutionary. Not in the shock and awe sense of the word, but in how it connects to experiences we all have had trying to understand and realize our sexual selves. With a background in psychiatry and medical biology, Madeleine's grasp on the subject of how to regain sexual intimacy with oneself and one's partner is uncanny. Reading her book promises to open up a both compassionate and deeply insightful perspective on how to make whole again an area in modern existence that has been overburdened by misconceptions and stigmas that block one of the -- if not THE -- most powerful sources of connection to the vitality that suffuses our experience of being alive and of loving."
- **Sayer Ji, Founder of GreenMedInfo.com**

"Dr Castellanos offers an accessible, honest look at the typical sexual struggles for modern couples. Her holistic treatment model expertly guides readers in understanding sexuality from a biological and emotional perspective, thus assisting them in creating a more satisfying sexual experience."

- Marianne Brandon, PhD, author of
Monogamy: The Untold Story

"It's as if you were a true insider into the dynamics fueling sexual dysfunctions. Dr. Castellanos provides a functional approach to major obstacles of sexual pleasure in an easy-to-understand format. It's a sneak peek into the major issues of sex therapy."

- Ian Kerner, author of *She Comes First*

Wanting to Want

Also by Madeleine M. Castellanos, M.D.

A Man's Guide to Male Sexual Issues
A Woman's Guide to Male Sexual Issues

WANTING TO WANT

What Kills Your Sex Life, and How to Keep It Alive

MADELEINE M. CASTELLANOS, M.D.

Tao Health

For all of my patients,
who show their bravery in confronting their fears,
and affirm the strength of their life force when they nurture
their sexual selves. You teach me each day what it means to be
alive.

Contents

Introduction

Having practiced sex therapy in New York City for over a decade, I can tell you that most people still aren't sure exactly what sex therapy is about. Besides fielding questions about how long therapy takes and what it entails, I've also had questions like, "Am I going to have to take my clothes off?"

Sex therapy is based on classic talk therapy, where the therapist and client explore all the factors that may be preventing a full expression of that person's sexuality. Although physical factors can play a major role in sexual dysfunction, psychological causes are actually more likely, and a combination of both factors is usually involved. It's not unheard of to see an eighty-year-old with plenty of sexual desire who enjoys his or her sex life, or instead a physically healthy twenty-five-year-old who is unable to find sexual pleasure either with a partner or alone. As a medical doctor (M.D.) specializing in psychiatry, I am in a unique position to help patients address both the physical and psychological aspects of sexual dysfunction. Interestingly, it's usually the psychological aspect that causes the most difficulty in the area of sexuality. Fortunately, gaining a better understanding of how those forces work, everyone can significantly improve his or her sex life.

It's not uncommon for people to enter into sex therapy with the romanticized hope that the therapist will utter a magical phrase that will somehow turn everything around for them. Part of this comes from feelings of helplessness and frustration in dealing with sexual difficulties. Part of it also comes from not being aware of the major factors that can derail one's sex life.

I am honored to be able to teach people about the makeup of their sexual nature and how they can improve their sex lives and relationships. Everything you have learned about sex over your lifetime, all your desires and curiosities, all the ways you like to express yourself sexually, and all the ways your personality is channeled through your sexual expression are all facets of your sexual self.

One of my passions is getting people in touch with their true natures, both physically and psychologically. When you get to know your sexual self and nurture and support it, you experience more pleasure and personal growth, not just in your sex life but in all areas of your life. This is why I want to give you some insight into the most common roadblocks to good sex. Since what you experience psychologically gets translated into your physical body, internal factors can often manifest as physical symptoms—a sign that your sexual self is trying to tell you something.

Much of the advice readily available about how to improve your sex life is focused on aspects outside of you—how to give oral sex, how to dress up date night, and ways to excite your partner. But based on my clinical experience with thousands of people, I can tell you that the biggest factors affecting your sex life come from within. Usually your own insecurities and fears and the limits of your comfort zone contribute more to the quality of your sexual pleasure than any external factors.

In this book, I want to introduce you to the factors I see most commonly in my practice that affect people's ability to have maximal sexual pleasure. Each of these can be a potential roadblock that keeps you from creating powerful, exciting experiences time after time. What you'll learn is very different from what the majority of sex advice offers because I'm not promising a quick fix. Instead, we'll take a good, hard look at the realities of our sexual nature, how it's influenced by our internal world, and how to work with it for a happy sex life.

The most common difficulties I see in my practice are problems with low sexual desire and problems with sexual arousal. There can be several different causes for problems with sexual desire, sexual arousal, and other sexual dysfunctions that people don't usually think about. Clients often lump together the difficulties of desire and arousal, especially since there is so much overlap between the two. In fact, desire and arousal can either reinforce each other or sabotage each other. When one is present, it usually affects the other.

The problem of low sexual desire is perhaps the most common sexual difficulty that I (and other therapists) see. Despite the hope for a simple answer, low sexual desire is an extremely complex dilemma. Sexual desire is dependent on the interplay of what's going on physically, psychologically, emotionally, and in relation to your partner. Of course, dissecting *the entire* web of interactions that take place to either boost or to ruin desire is beyond the scope of this book. Instead, I want to give an honest and approachable look at the things you can do today to give you maximum sexual pleasure for a long-lasting sex life.

Chapter 1

How to Conceptualize Sexual Difficulties

There she sits in my office, poised apprehensively at the edge of the couch. I encourage her to sit back, to take a few deep, relaxing breaths, and to tell me what she is coming into treatment for at this time. Married for five years, but together with her partner for a total of seven, Julie is a thin, energetic woman with an unassuming way about her.

She starts shyly. "I just don't understand why, but I really find it difficult to want to have sex with my husband." I ask her for more details, and she lets out a soft, nervous giggle.

"I don't know why. He's a great guy, and I love him very much. I just don't really get excited about wanting to have sex with him. I feel bad for him and for me too. I don't know what's wrong with me. I just want to want, you know?"

The one question I am asked more often than any other question related to sex is how to get sexual desire to last. Problems with low sexual desire plague a majority of people at some time during their lives and often in spite of loving their partner. It's such a common dilemma that a whole market exists for products designed specifically to enhance sexual desire or to "bring the spark back into your relationship." Products that boost libido make up a multibillion-dollar business, whether they work or not. But it almost doesn't matter whether they work, because what they are really selling is hope—the possibility that your sexual desire and sex life will be instantly revived.

So what is happening to sexual desire in the sex lives of millions and millions of people? Why is it so difficult to keep that same thrill and excitement over time, even with the best of partners? It's not just an isolated problem for a select few. Studies suggest that from 26 percent to 52 percent of women have difficulty with low sexual desire at some point in their lives, depending on their age[1], and about 13 percent to 28 percent of men do too.[2]

Many people wonder if there is something wrong with them, and they just want to feel normal again. Others are convinced that they aren't attracted to their partner anymore and give up. For many, it becomes easier to ignore the problem; they convince themselves that they don't need sex in their lives or that they just aren't very sexual. There is such a thing as *asexual* people (people who have never had sexual desires), but they make up a very small percentage of the population—just 1 percent to 2 percent. That is not who I see in my office, and it is certainly not Julie.

As I start to think about the difficulty that Julie is having with not wanting to have sex with her husband, I want to make sure to cover all the bases, including everything from where she learned about sex to the details of her sexual activity with her husband. I ask her to tell me about their sex life in the beginning of their relationship and how she felt about it then.

"Well, we used to have sex all the time—not much got in our way. It was a lot of fun, and it just seemed really easy to be with each other, you know?" A sad look comes across her face as she talks about the changes in her life in the years that followed—moving to a city that she feels is too big for her and the birth of twin boys, now almost four years old.

Throughout telling me her history, Julie tries to reassure me, and probably herself at the same time, that "I really do love him, though! It's not that he's not attractive. I just always find reasons not to have sex."

Julie's story is all too common nowadays. Her lack of sexual desire is a symptom of some other underlying difficulty that she and I still haven't discovered. In thinking about how to approach Julie's predicament, I keep in mind that there could be many different paths that brought her here today. In fact, a combination of several factors probably led her to this pattern with her husband.

As a physician, I understand how much complexity goes into the physical aspects of sexual desire. But as a psychiatrist, I have also come to appreciate the multitude of psychological and emotional factors that help shape and modulate sexual desire. This means that there are many forces working together to enhance sexual desire—or working against each other to make it more difficult to attain. My task is to find out just what those different forces are and help Julie and her husband separate those that enhance desire from those that lessen desire so they can create new patterns that are more suited to a happy sex life for them.

More than ever, science has an understanding of how the brain learns and changes over time, depending on your patterns of thinking and your patterns of behavior. When it comes to sexual desire, the brain can actually learn not to want sex for various reasons. Maybe you don't get as much enjoyment out of it compared to how much effort you put into it? Perhaps there has been pain or discomfort, and now your mind is trying to avoid experiencing that discomfort again?

There are several dimensions of sexual desire outside of the physical that have to align for healthy sexual desire, such as what you have learned about what's sexually appropriate, how you feel about yourself sexually, and what you interpret in your partner as being sexy, to name a few. Yet Julie was perplexed as to what could be happening and even had difficulty remembering what sex was like when she had it.

When I asked her just how often she was having sex, she said "I don't know really. I guess about once a month, maybe longer than that."

So that began our exploration to find the source of her difficulties—was it something that was draining her desire for sex, or was there something she was trying to avoid that manifested as low desire?

Whenever there is sexual dysfunction, it's important to focus on sexual pleasure. By itself, pleasure is a delicious reward for any activity, sex included. But what happens in your brain when there is less pleasure, or when you are distracted from pleasure? How does this affect the desire for future sexual experiences?

People often underestimate the effect that diminished sexual pleasure has on sexual desire. In this book, I want to share with you some common issues that many people don't automatically associate with problems in sexual functioning or low sexual desire, but they are present in every relationship in one way or another.

THE MULTIPLE DIMENSIONS OF SEXUAL DESIRE

So far, Julie has told us that at the beginning of her relationship, she used to have sex with her husband all the time, and that it was fun for her. She also has talked about being somewhat unhappy with living in the city. We know that she is attracted to her husband, but we still don't have any information about her relationship with her boys, or about how life changed for her after their birth. All of these details and more will help shed light on her difficulty with libido.

For Julie, and for almost every other patient that walks through my door, there is no *one* issue that is the cause of sexual difficulties. Instead, the interaction of many different forces in combination over time has zapped her desire to have sex with her husband. Each aspect of your being affects the other. The physical affects the psychological, which in turn then affects the physical. The emotional is constantly being expressed in all the tissues of the body, such as when depression slows down the immune system[3] or how emotional vitality can lower your risk for coronary artery disease.[4] Spirituality also has physical manifestations in the flesh and has been demonstrated to decrease medical symptoms.[5]

Our sexuality cannot be separated from any other part of ourselves. A person's sexuality is made up of *every* aspect of their being. This means that whether you think so or not, your sexuality also affects you physically, psychologically, and socially (in your relations to other people). Thus, I like to break down sexual difficulties into those three dimensions.

Physical or Biological Dimension

Most people look for a physical reason why their sex life has fizzled. Of course, there may be very distinct physical reasons for having sexual difficulties. Hormones can play a significant role in your energy level, your responsiveness, and your interest. But hormones aren't limited to just estrogen and testosterone. Other hormones such as cortisol, progesterone, DHEA, thyroid, and insulin all play their part in healthy sexual desire and sexual functioning. All these hormones work in harmony with each other to create a balance where both the body and the mind are working together efficiently, which is the groundwork for good sex.

It's tempting to think that if a little hormone is good for you, then more will be better. When it comes to the delicate hormonal balance in the body, however, this isn't the case. Your body is constantly keeping tabs on your hormone levels and adjusting them as it sees fit. Low levels of a certain hormone usually indicate some imbalance in the body that has a deeper cause.

It's also important to keep in mind that the body gives priority to healthy levels of several other hormones before it deals with the sex hormones (estrogen, testosterone, and progesterone). As far as the body is concerned, cortisol will always be number one. Cortisol not only helps regulate energy availability for the body, but along with adrenaline, it is also secreted as part of the fight-or-flight response to stress. The body protects its production of cortisol for times of stress and will actually decrease production of the sex hormones if it's under too much stress. Next in line, the body prioritizes the thyroid and thyroid hormones over the sex hormones, because the thyroid is what modulates metabolism, thus keeping you alive.

In Chapter 7, I will cover the physical (biological) reasons why a person may have low sexual dysfunction. As you can see, it's not as simple as just giving estrogen and testosterone. Many physical factors together play a role. That includes sleep, nutrition, alcohol use, drugs, exercise, and even sexual activity itself. You have quite a bit of control over all of these factors, which means that you can directly affect your sex life by optimizing your physical lifestyle.

In Julie's case, I have to examine her medical history, including what medications she takes now and has taken in the past.

"I used to take birth control pills, up until the time that we decided to try to get pregnant—which ended up being right away," she said. "I started back up again after the boys were a few months old."

A history of hormonal birth control points to a possible imbalance in her hormones due to the pill's overall effect on testosterone—something I'll have to investigate a little further by testing hormone levels in the blood. A more detailed history of how she actually feels physically during sex is also going to be very important to flesh out any physical causes for her low sex drive. I'd like to know, for example, if she has lost sensation in her genitals, or worse, is she experiencing any discomfort or pain with sex?

Psychological Dimension

The physical aspect of sex is only one dimension of sexual desire and activity. There are much stronger forces at work when it comes to sexual functioning in humans. For animals, sex operates on a seasonal schedule that is ruled by hormones and instinct. Humans, on the other hand, have sex and sexual desire at all times during the year and during a woman's cycle. They are not reigned in simply by changes in hormones. Instead, psychological factors exert a considerable influence on sexual desire and activity and can completely overrule what the hormones have to say.

Everything that you are taught about sex and sexuality from the time you're born helps make up your ideas about sex. Learning what is sexy versus what is disgusting is something that happens in your childhood and teen years, shaping the list of what will become a turn-on or a turnoff for you. These ideas about what is sexy and what isn't are heavily shaped by culture and by how others around you respond to different aspects of sex and sexuality. They even affect how you think of your body and your sexual functioning—whether something is appropriate or not—which then affects how much pleasure you allow yourself to feel.

How does Julie feel about sexual activity and what does it mean to her? How does she feel about her own sexuality and her body? Did she learn to be guilty about her sex or her sexual thoughts? Does she allow herself to fantasize, or does she find her fantasies improper, embarrassing, or worse, a betrayal of her husband?

The psychological forces at play when it comes to sex can be greater than the physical ones. Since your brain processes every little bit of information it receives, it acts as a gatekeeper to the deeper parts of your primitive brain where sexual arousal is controlled. The thinking part of your brain decides if something is sexy or not, and then either allows the arousal process to continue, or short-circuits it. Even before you get to arousal, the thinking part of your brain is controlling sexual desire. In fact, it's the one that decides if it's appropriate for you to have desire, if you deserve desire, if you think desire will bring you a reward, or whether you should feel guilty for having desire. The thinking brain then decides if it's going to allow arousal to proceed. These are just some of the ways that the thinking brain can rule your sex life.

Social Dimension

"So how is the rest of the relationship with your husband aside from sex?" I asked Julie.

"It's okay, I guess. I just get upset with him sometimes because I don't think he understands what it's like to take care of two twin boys; it's like I have to do everything. And even when he does help out, he only does things halfway. No matter what, I end up taking care of them and then taking care of him too. I wish he would get that."

Julie has some definite sore points in her relationship with her husband that are, without a doubt, contributing to her overall picture of low libido. It would be unreasonable to expect that she could completely separate how she feels about her caregiving duties from her sexual feelings for her husband.

Because sexual desire and longing are usually felt toward another person (although there is sexual desire for masturbation, which is healthy and normal), it's important to consider all of the social factors that tie into that relationship. If you are in a relationship, the most obvious factor is how you feel toward your partner and how you interact with them. Are you happy with them? Do you want to please them? Do you think they want the best for you? All these questions and more affect how you experience being with them, and ultimately, your continued sexual desire for them.

For Julie, it was important to distinguish between the desire for sex with her husband and sexual activity by herself—or masturbation.

"I don't have any problems with masturbation. I like it, and I orgasm every time, sometimes a couple of times. I would say I do it a couple of times a week." Julie reported.

I asked her, "How do you decide that you're going to masturbate?"

With a little puzzled look on her face, she said, "I either just get the thought in my head, or I feel like I want to in my body."

All of this information points to a woman with active sexual feelings and desires. And clearly, she is having sexual activity on her own. But something is keeping her from experiencing the desire to have sex with her husband.

When thinking about the social dimension of your sex life, it's almost impossible to completely separate the many different factors involved. There may be some crossover between the social and the psychological, the psychological and the physical, or the physical and the social. It can be almost impossible to tease out and separate the different factors affecting one another. It's more important to first recognize that it's happening and then find out how to change things to your advantage.

For example, if you're tired after a long day at work, your partner has been a little grumpy with you ever since you got home, and you're very stressed about an early morning presentation that may mean a promotion, you may not have much desire for sex that night. The physical reality of being tired and stressed will have a negative impact on your body, but so will any anger or distance from your partner, as well as your desire to impress your boss at the job. Recognizing each of these details helps you decide which factor needs to be addressed first, or if any or all can be overcome at that moment at all.

So you see, you are much more complex when it comes to your sexuality and sexual desire than any other animal in the animal kingdom. When thinking about the causes of sexual difficulties, you have to consider the physical, the psychological, and the social aspects together to get a complete picture. In Julie's case, clearly there's still a lot of information to find out about her and her sexual relationship with her husband. We'll get back to Julie a little later.

I am a firm believer in addressing the root cause of a problem. In my practice, I don't jump to prescribe hormones or medications for sexual functioning without finding out what else is happening in the relationship. Unless the underlying cause is handled first, the issue will continue to get more and more involved, and the person will get increasingly stuck in their sexual difficulties. Whatever is dampening a person's natural desire and arousal must be corrected if they want long-lasting results (and no side effects).

I also believe, as stated earlier, that the psychological and relational aspects of sexual functioning are oftentimes more powerful than the physical aspect. Therefore, the following chapters will examine the most common psychological and relational factors I have seen in my practice that can impact your sex life. The last chapter will be devoted to physical considerations when examining sexual dysfunction. I place the nonphysical factors first because I want to stress how important I think they are, and how they can directly influence sexual desire and sexual functioning on a whole.

Things to consider:

- *How do you think about your own sexuality? Is it something positive and valuable in your eyes, or do you think that it's problematic, dirty, or unwanted?*

- *Do you think that a person should automatically get turned on with certain stimulation, like when a guy sees a naked woman, or when a woman has her breasts fondled?*

- *Do you expect your body to respond to sex automatically regardless of how you treat it—poor sleep, junk food, smoking, and so forth?*

- *When thinking about your overall health, do you consider your sexuality to play a major role in your physical and psychological health? Or do you see those aspects of health as separate?*

- *What has changed in your life that could be affecting your sexual functioning and desire for sex?*

Chapter 2

How Disconnection and Dissociation Affect Sex and Desire

Meet Melissa, a thirty-four-year-old mother of two (a six-year-old boy and a girl aged three and a half), who keeps herself relatively fit, and loves and is attracted to her husband. She is coming into therapy because she finds that she is not really interested in sex, and more often than not, she thinks that having sex isn't worth the trouble. Despite this, she feels a sense of obligation to her husband and wishes that she was as interested in sex as she used to be at the beginning of their relationship.

Upon inquiring, I find that Melissa has been working a full-time job doing office work for a small business in the city for the last year and half. Although she is fortunate to have the children in day care and school now, she feels guilty about not having enough time to spend with them as she used to and feels that she has to split her time between the children and her husband. He does try to help out, but the kids seem to be more demanding of her and her time. When it comes to the end of the night, it's an effort for her and her husband to get the kids to bed on schedule so they can have some time alone together.

I asked Melissa what goes through her mind when she is finally in bed and her husband starts to come on to her. She answers:

"I have a hard time focusing. I think about what I have to do the next day, what time I need to get up to get the kids ready for school, and then my mind wanders to thoughts about work and the day. Worse is when I start thinking about how terrible I feel that I don't really care if we have sex or not."

When I ask her how she feels in her body when her husband starts touching her, she says "Really? I feel numb. I feel the opposite of sexy. I feel nothing. It's like it doesn't even register with me."

Melissa is caught in a loop of feeling distracted (by her kids and her work) and disconnected (from her husband) when it comes to sexual pleasure and desire. She doesn't identify any desire within herself when her husband comes on to her, and even finds it difficult to feel much when he touches and kisses her.

Scenarios like Melissa's are not uncommon in people's busy lives today. Although many people identify with Melissa's feelings, most don't really know how they got there in the first place. The demanding life of a working mom can spell disaster for an active and enjoyable sex life. But it's not just working moms that find themselves in this predicament— anyone can fall prey to distraction and stress taking them away from connecting to their sexual pleasure and desire.

DISCONNECTION

Disconnection happens over time when the body's messages are put on the backburner to make room for other things that the mind considers a higher priority at the moment. Here, I am specifically talking about messages related to sexual stimulation and activity, but they could be any messages sent from the body, like hunger, restlessness, or even fatigue. After continuing to ignore the body's messages, you become less attuned to them, and this creates a loop of further distance from the pleasurable experience of sex.

You are able to enjoy a greater amount of sexual pleasure when you are really tuned in to all of the pleasurable sensations you are experience during sex, and when you allow those sensations to build your arousal. Anything that causes a disconnect—distraction or anxious worrying—can interfere with that focus, deafening the signal to pleasure, which then muffles sexual arousal.

Unfortunately, many people already have some level of disconnect between what their body is experiencing and what their brain is registering. This results in your brain tuning out a big chunk of pleasurable and erotic sensations. They are literally blocked out by your brain because your brain has either developed a pattern of ignoring those signals from the body, discounted those signals as unimportant, or interpreted them as uncomfortable and related to anxiety and therefore looks for other sensations to focus on instead. This is how anxiety and distraction can actually cause you to *feel less*. A good example of distraction leading to disconnection is how a toddler can easily forget about a scraped knee if her attention is refocused on getting back to the playground rather than on thinking about the fall she just had.

Disconnection can be thought of as distance between what your body is experiencing and what your brain is registering. When a person has some level of being disconnected from their body, they aren't capable of fully listening to what their body is telling them. They may have lost the ability to read the signals their body sends them, like when a person becomes deaf to the body's signal of thirst—if staying well hydrated and using the bathroom frequently is very inconvenient for them at their job. Another example of disconnecting from the body's signals is when a person interprets a heavy feeling in their legs from sitting all day long as fatigue, when in fact it's really the body's cry for more movement.

When such a disconnection occurs during sex, it may mean that while one individual is kissing or rubbing against their partner, they may not have a very high level of excitement, or they may feel that the physical part of it is just "okay." It's what Melissa was describing when she said she felt "numb."

To make matters worse, the brain may even be coming up with lots of negative thoughts during sexual activity and focusing on those rather than on any pleasure or excitement. This tends to lead people to cast a negative shadow over the entire experience and short-circuit any chance for a high level of arousal. When this happens time and again, the brain learns to turn off sexual desire because sex doesn't lead to as much pleasure as it used to.

Take Steven, for example. He is a healthy twenty-seven-year-old man with a good job in finances and fairly confident when it comes to his work. He enjoys going to shows and being social with his friends both in and out of town. The one area he just can't seem to make work is his sex life.

"I really want to be able to have sex, but I just can't rely on getting an erection. Or if I get one, I'm always worried that I'm going to lose it, and then I usually do." I'm to the point now where I don't even want to go on a date because I think it's going to be a problem."

Steven has fallen into a loop of negative thoughts driving higher and higher levels of anxiety. He is disconnected from how his body is feeling at the moment of sexual stimulation, and instead he is caught up in his head, focused on his performance rather than his pleasure. Each time he has an anxious thought, it reinforces an entire anxious pattern of thinking that triggers a stress response—the direct opposite of what's needed for sexual arousal and a good erection. This pattern has grown into a vicious circle of negative thoughts and doubts about his ability to "perform." And these negative thoughts form a type of distraction and disconnection from any positive feelings or thoughts he could be having with a partner.

When I asked Steven how it felt in his body to get an erection, his answer was "I don't really notice feeling anything." It wasn't until I started drawing his attention back to his physical sensations that he became more aware of them. He was so preoccupied with his performance and the negative thoughts driving his anxiety that he had forgotten to enjoy all of the physical pleasure available to him.

For Steven, it was particularly important to address his negative automatic thoughts that were not only increasing his anxiety, but also acting as a distraction from any sexy thoughts he could have been having. Special attention in the form of cognitive behavioral therapy was needed to help him mold his thought patterns so that he could quickly and effectively handle the negative thoughts before they turned into a cascade of negativity that would ruin the moment. In Chapter 7, we'll see how this anxious pattern of thinking was connected to his ability to get and keep his erection.

Disconnection due to distraction can be particularly common for women. In fact, many women don't even recognize they have sexual desire unless they are first experiencing sexual arousal[6]. Women's brains in particular are wired to pay attention to a large amount of detail at any one time. This means that when it comes to sex, there seems to be a lot more chatter going on in their heads, making it more difficult to focus on the pleasure[7]. Not only does this "chatter" interfere with sexual desire, but it can lengthen the amount of time it takes to get aroused and significantly impact a woman's ability to reach orgasm.

For Melissa, the disconnection resulted in sex feeling much less pleasurable. Each time she would have sex in a disconnected fashion, her brain would take notes and associate sex with a numb feeling. In this way, she quickly taught herself to be disinterested in sex without meaning to. The result was a lack of sexual desire and feeling that sex wasn't worth the trouble.

A mind-body disconnect, at least to some degree, is not uncommon for men and women alike. When you are born, you pay 100 percent attention to what your body is telling you all the time. As you learn that there are other people and things in the world, you start to focus your attention outward. As soon as you are taught language, disconnection becomes more common because you are taught that words and thoughts carry more weight than your gut feelings do. You also learn to betray your feelings and your body when, as children, adults tell you that you don't really feel the way you think you do.

For example, how many of you have heard these kinds of statements as a child:

"Don't cry. You shouldn't feel sad."

"Don't tell me you're not cold. Put on a sweater."

Or something as innocent as:

"I know you have to go to the bathroom, but you will have to hold it."

All these statements help teach you to ignore what your body is telling you—whether it's for your good or not. When this happens, you stop listening to the signals your body is sending in order to pay attention to something else, like whether you will get scolded if you can't wait to use the bathroom, or anything else besides the feeling of your sweater against your warm skin.

In sex, when you stop paying attention fully to the body's messages, you only process part of the information being sent from your body to your brain. When you miss out on any sensual information, or filter out pleasure, you can't get the full effect of pleasure, because you're not completely paying attention to it.

How to Improve Disconnectedness

Simply being disconnected from what your body is feeling can be greatly improved and eventually overcome with attention to bodily sensations and sensual experiences in any of your five senses. This is really just mindfulness around the signals that your body is sending you, and what you are experiencing from moment to moment. In this way, you strengthen the mind-body connection and let in more information from your senses. This lets you focus on the pleasure without blocking out part, or all of it, so that you can get the full effect of your lover's touch.

Our busy world encourages people to quickly shift their attention from one task to the next, never fully paying attention to one thing in particular. One exercise that I often give my patients is to hold a simple object in their hand, like a shell, a pen, or a coin. Next, I tell them to focus on that object for three minutes, taking notice of every little characteristic and detail. When they find their attention wandering (as it often does), I encourage them not to reproach themselves, but simply to bring their attention back to the object and continue as before. Although the exercise is not very complex, it can involve a considerable amount of effort if a person is not used to focusing their attention for very long. It can be stretched out to five or ten minutes for even more practice. Even the distractions can be useful, because each time a person brings their attention back to the object, the brain learns to increase it's flexibility.

DISSOCIATION

Dissociation is a much more intense form of disconnection. It's when a person may not have a sense of their body at all, or may feel as if they're floating outside their body. When a person dissociates, they may not even fully respond to others; they may look "zoned out" or like they are in a trance. There are different levels of dissociation, some more severe than others, but basically, it makes you unaware of what you're feeling and experiencing at the moment.

Dissociation is the mind's way of protecting itself from being overwhelmed. Unlike disconnection, dissociation normally doesn't take place in a person's development unless there has been some sort of trauma or some very intense feelings that the person was unable to process at the time they happened. This can lead to episodes of dissociation in order to protect the person from the intense feelings. Unfortunately, if a person continues to dissociate, especially in matters related to physical intimacy, they will be unable to participate in sexual pleasure with their partner under that state.

If a person is dissociating during sex, they are experiencing a high level of anxiety, whether they are aware of it or not. In the attempt to not feel pain or extremely uncomfortable feelings, dissociation doesn't allow a person to feel at all. Some people may even find themselves observing their actions as if they were outside their own body. Others just seem to be in a state that feels more like hypnosis—numb to whatever is going on around them.

Some causes of dissociation are prior sexual abuse, intense social anxiety or fear of intimacy, or engaging in actions that are strongly opposed to one's beliefs. When a person is dissociated, they not only are separated from what they are experiencing, but they are unable to think or work with those feelings in the moment either.

How to Heal from Dissociation

Dissociation is much trickier to resolve and requires more extensive therapy in order to process certain emotions. Learning little by little to tolerate more intense emotions will allow you to participate in a greater range of emotions, including sexual pleasure and joy.

Increase the connection with your body by doing daily exercises in mindfulness and sensuality (see below). Even though these exercises only take a few minutes a day, they must be practiced continually to re-establish and strengthen the mind-body connection. This will increase your sexual pleasure in the moment as well as add to your motivation and desire for sex in the future.

Ways to increase your sexual pleasure in the moment include:

- *Notice the feel of your skin as you soap yourself up in the shower.*

- *Practice abdominal breathing, feeling the breath going in and out as you inhale and exhale.*

- *Sit with your thoughts without any tech device and just see what comes to your mind. Don't fight the thoughts, just be aware of them.*

- *See if you can sense your heartbeat—you can use your hand over your chest to find it first and then try sensing it without your hand.*

- *Focus on the sensation of warmth or vibration in your genitals the next time you start to feel sexual arousal either with a partner or by yourself.*

Chapter 3

Expectations and Sexual Pleasure

We have seen how disconnection can interfere with recognizing pleasure at the physical level. Now let's examine how your expectations can interfere with recognizing pleasure at the level of your mind.

Expectations are any thoughts you have about any aspect or detail of a situation. When you anticipate something, have an opinion about it, or have feelings related to it, you create an expectation of what you will experience. It is a natural part of how your brain works—comparing experiences you are having to what you have experienced before, either by yourself directly or based on what others have told you.

Although expectations are a normal part of your brain's functioning, they don't always work to your advantage. Positive or negative expectations can influence an experience by either enhancing it, ruining it, or any point in between. Depending on what you are expecting, you either open your mind up to an experience or shut yourself off from it. Expectations set you up for wonderment or for disappointment. They basically tell your brain not only what it should want, but also to be unsatisfied if you don't get what you expect.

Expectations are so powerful that they can even change the way you perceive sensations traveling through your nervous system. This was cleverly demonstrated through an elegant study in which patients were submitted to exactly the same physical sensation of pressure, but felt more or less pain depending on whether they were told, respectively, to expect their pain to increase or that they were being given a painkiller (when it was really a placebo).[8]

Other studies have shown that people rate a wine as better tasting with an overall heightened sensation of pleasure if they believe that the wine they are tasting is expensive.[9] In both of these experiments, the experience was altered because the expectation carried the power of suggestion. Not only did each of these studies speak to the dramatic effect of expectations, but they also demonstrated activation of chemicals related to pleasure and/or stress as a result of those expectations. They show that there is a physical change created by an expectation that determines how you will perceive any experience.

Unfortunately, expectations are commonly to blame for sexual dissatisfaction. Sexual desire in humans is much more complex than a simple instinctual response ruled by hormones, the time of year, and the strict behavioral patterns as seen in other animals. Humans have all of these influences, of course. But we also have a much larger layer of emotion and meaning that is attached to our sexual interactions and significantly shapes our thoughts, preferences, and desires. Many of these ideas are passed on in our culture, through our family, through images and messages in advertising and movies, and through what we learn from religion, teachers, and friends. Each person also has their own personal level of meaning for what is sexy and appropriate, and their individual fantasies, wants, and pleasures are shaped by these. All of these can contribute to expectations that alter your experiences by creating a filter so that the brain only pays attention or gives importance to the particular behaviors, characteristics, or meanings it's looking for.

One of the main difficulties with expectations is that they are often unrealistic. Whether they are positive or negative, they're usually focused on a narrow range of experience and leave out realistic details. An example might be thinking about a first date and focusing on all the details of what your partner might say or do, but leaving out anything that you wouldn't really like. Or in the case of negative expectations, you might expect that a conversation with someone will be very unpleasant, so you actually tune out to anything that might be positive about the interaction.

When you see reality shows with celebrities boasting about how passionately they feel toward their partners or how "in love" they are, it's almost impossible not to automatically compare your relationship to theirs. Most people view shows, movies, and social media as indication or proof of what is going on in other people's lives, and there is almost always a subconscious pull to see how you compare. What happens then is that people's expectations of what relationships *should be like* starts to get based on what they *think* other people are experiencing or feeling. This is true whether it's your cousin on Facebook, a celebrity on a reality show, or a fictional character in a movie. What you see over and over shapes your expectations, and you compare yourself to see just how you measure up.

It is normal for your brain to behave this way—searching its environment to see what others are doing and then seeing how you compare. After all, from day one of life, each and every one of us learns from imitating the people around us. It's how you learn language, how to walk, how to behave, and what behaviors get the most reaction from others. You even have special neurons in your brain set up specifically for imitating other people's actions and feelings. They are called mirror neurons, and they encourage you to literally mirror what you see in others. Now just imagine that from the very first day you were born, your brain is encouraging you to "try on" other people's emotions and behaviors—sort of like a person tries on a sweater. Each time this happens, the brain takes notes until eventually it has learned how to do it on its own. Mirror neurons play a crucial role in learning and make the brain work very efficiently and fast.

But what is your brain exposed to? In the case of movies, television shows, and social media, the answer is information that is the most dramatic, extreme, or idealized stuff out there. It's no mystery that this is the content that keeps people interested, sells lots of products, and gets the most engagement from an audience. But the most fantastic, sugarcoated, perfect situations are not what most of life is about. The realities of day-to-day life include disappointment, imperfection, struggles, compromises, and boredom. People's lives are filled with downtime, routine, and effort—not usually the things glorified and promoted on reality TV or Pinterest. Sex is no exception.

Today, porn has also become a significant influence on shaping people's expectations about sex and sexual relationships. Not only do more children grow up with exposure to pornography than ever before, but many consider it a realistic view of normal sexual behavior (which it is not). In this way, porn comes to shape their expectations around sex. Porn can add a great deal of eroticism into one's sex life precisely because it is about fantasy. The trouble is that porn can create unrealistic expectations of what bodies should look like, how people naturally respond to different sexual stimulation, and what normal sexual behavior really is.

This is exactly what happened with a very young couple who came to see me, upset that sex just wasn't working the way it should. Andrea, twenty, and Bob, twenty-two, had been dating just a few months and each had only had one other sexual experience. They were frustrated and dissatisfied, often confused as to why they were so unhappy in their sex life. I asked them to describe the difficulty they were having.

Bob started, "I don't think that Andrea really likes sex, or at least sex with me. She doesn't get very excited and I feel like she doesn't really want me."

Andrea described a very different experience, "I guess that there must be something wrong with my vagina because I don't really get wet right away. I used to like the way that Bob felt, but now it's just more uncomfortable than it used to be. I also think that maybe I'm just not that sexual because I don't really get excited like other women do."

When I asked about who these other women were, she said that she had seen the other women Bob had shown her on porn, and it certainly was not how she was feeling. She was convinced that she just didn't get very excited.

Porn is an exaggeration of reality that plays on fantasy. It cannot include the complexities and nuances of human interactions around and during sex. It makes sex simplistic and straightforward, which it rarely ever is. Porn encourages people to expect sex to be void of discomfort, disagreements, or disappointment. With these expectations, you can develop a very narrow filter from which to view sex. To be fair, school, religion, parents, movies, romantic novels, or even conversations with your friends may create expectations that can be just as unrealistic and damaging as porn.

Unrealistic expectation can affect your sex life by influencing your ideas about sex directly, as well as by how you think the nature of your relationship with your partner should be. Modern-day partners are expected to fill the role of lover, best friend, business partner, soul mate, co-parent, and intellectual stimulant. But relationships did not always carry so much pressure. With the expectation that your partner will be all things to you at all times, you can easily get disillusioned that maybe they aren't the right one for you, or that you are missing out.

Such expectations make the brain hypersensitive to all the things that don't match up—to anything that you feel is negative or falls short. This creates a situation in which you are much more likely to discount or ignore positive things about your partner or your relationship. Interestingly, when you practice feeling gratitude toward your partner, you start to notice more positive aspects of both the person and the relationship.[10] In this way, gratitude counteracts unrealistic expectations and can strengthen loving feelings toward them.

When you develop an expectation about something, your mind paints a picture, not just of how it thinks something *will* be, but also how it thinks it *should* be. This is especially true for sex because it has such a personal meaning. Your brain then automatically compares the actual experience you have to the imagined or expected experience. And anything that doesn't match up, it either disregards or tries to explain away. If you expect something to be the ideal situation, your actual experience usually falls short of it. If you're expecting something to be very negative, your brain looks for exactly the information that confirms your belief.

While all this is going on, your brain also tends to block out any information that doesn't match up to what it has been expecting. Sometimes, it doesn't even register the information. This is exactly how magicians and con men pull off their tricks. Trouble is, in sex, when your brain isn't paying attention to something or is interpreting it negatively, you can't build up the experience of pleasure enough to fuel arousal.

When you focus heavily on predetermined expectations, you limit your brain's ability to focus on your actual experience and its ability to fully take in all the sensations in an objective way. So by comparing something to a hypothetical that doesn't actually exist at that moment, you filter out part of the information you are receiving from what's actually happening.

The same thing happens in your sex life. Regardless of where they come from, expectations about what you think sex *should* look like, feel like, sound like, or smell like will affect the way you experience sex with your partner. You may even form expectations about how your partner should act and what it all means. Overreaching or unrealistic expectations set you up for disappointment and frustration— not very erotic for any relationship.

Performance anxiety is one of those things fueled by expectations. If you think that you will fail at something and then be judged or embarrassed, you have already put that negative expectation in your mind. It then becomes the overriding belief, which can literally paralyze you. Performance anxiety in the bedroom comes in the form of erectile dysfunction, difficulty lubricating, or even difficulty reaching orgasm.

Unrealistic and negative expectations are what were causing Bob and Andrea to have such a difficult time. First of all, they both had the expectation that a woman should be able to get excited for sex, mentally and physically, pretty quickly. From watching examples in porn, they had come to believe that it was normal for women to get lubricated easily, even with a minimal amount of physical stimulation. Porn, of course, doesn't include a whole lot of psychological stimulation between partners, so it was impossible for them to judge what role that played in a woman's arousal.

Next, they also had the impression that women were very excited throughout the entire act of sex because of the strong reactions they noticed from women in porn. They also assumed that every woman would be just as vocal about their excitement as what they saw in porn. It's not that women can't get to very high levels of excitement—of course they can, and often do—but it seemed so automatic and continuous in porn that Bob wasn't sure if Andrea was aroused at all, and Andrea even started to doubt her own level of arousal.

All that doubt soon became a self-fulfilling chain reaction. Pretty soon, the worry and negativity created by their expectations led to more negativity that translated into Andrea being less excited overall. They were allowing the external measure of porn to shape their expectations of sex, which they could never live up to comfortably.

For Andrea and Bob, solid information about sex and their own sexual responses was what they needed. Once they had permission to think about sex in a different way and then were able to be curious about each other rather than more critical, they found that there was quite a bit of excitement, pleasure, and yes—lubrication. They were able to see their true sexual selves in sex rather than continuously compare themselves to actors hamming it up for the camera. Andrea, especially, went through a short period of anxiety that Bob might not love or accept her in her true sexual expression. But as she was more able to focus on her pleasure, he learned to enjoy what a high level of arousal looked like in his partner.

CHALLENGING YOUR EXPECTATIONS

The best way to stop predetermined expectations from souring your enjoyment of sex is to challenge those expectations. Ask yourself, "Where did these ideas come from: the movies, porn, my friends telling stories, a past lover?" If so, remember that not only is each person different, but each combination of lovers is different, and even each experience with one person can be different from one day to another. Next, focus on each experience as a new set of sensations. Be curious about each and every sensation, movement, and feeling. Each moment is unique and you deserve to experience the full pleasure of it by being as open to pleasure as you can be. In sex, it's less about what's right or wrong, and more about what's right for you.

It's important to remember that what you hope for and what you expect are two different things, and you should not confuse one with the other. Hopes and aspirations are ambitions and goals that allow you to plan and motivate yourself for the future. There is room for flexibility and adjustment when it comes to hopes and aspirations, whereas expectations tend to make you less flexible and accommodating.

You can challenge expectations by doing the following:

- *Ask yourself: "Where did this idea about sex come from in my life? Are my ideas about sex hurting me or limiting me in any way?"*

- *Find out how others have adopted their expectations about sex.*

- *Consider if your expectations are making you more anxious or unhappy.*

- *If you are honest with yourself, what is the worst thing that would happen if you challenged your expectations about sex?*

- *Think about whether you are judging yourself too harshly and how it may be sabotaging your intimacy.*

- *Remind yourself that through your expectations about sex, you create your own reality for your sex life and your sexuality overall.*

- *Take a few minutes each day to write down something that you feel grateful for in your relationship and your sex life.*

Chapter 4

You Are Responsible for Your Sexual Arousal

So many people seem to give their power away when it comes to sexuality. Whenever someone says "I want my partner to turn me on," it shows that they believe that what another person looks likes, or says, or does has more power to turn them on than their own thoughts. This is really part of a greater issue of not taking responsibility for what you think or feel. It's seen in medicine all the time—via the message that is constantly promoted to patients: "Just take this pill to take care of your symptoms." Not only does this message encourage people not to take responsibility for their health overall, but it also seems to put the power in someone else's or some thing's hands.

When you mistakenly place responsibility for your sexual arousal on your partner, it's easy to forget that the reason that you find your partner sexy or exciting is because of how *you* interpret that person's physique or actions. How you think about what's happening is what really determines what is arousing to you—which is why you will always hear sex therapists and educators say that the brain is the largest sex organ in the body. You won't experience sexual pleasure and arousal unless your brain permits them to take place.

What this means is that arousal happens first inside your head in response to what happens in your outside world. So where your thoughts go determines if you get turned on in your body or not. Are you taking the responsibility to focus on what is erotic for you? Do you allow yourself to think about those things that are the sexiest and most arousing to you during sex? Are you giving away your sexual power by waiting for your partner to give you pleasure rather than seeking out your pleasure at any given moment? Or maybe you fill your mind with pressure, guilt, and frustration because you feel responsible for how your partner feels and for their happiness in sex?

Remember Melissa who just felt "numb?" Besides being somewhat disconnected from her body, she was waiting for her husband to make her feel differently. She had not noticed how her increased responsibilities in her growing family had taken her thoughts away from sexual pleasure. But because she didn't know that all of that power was inside her own mind, she started to worry that she wasn't attracted to her husband anymore and so he just didn't "do it" for her.

By addressing the combination of disconnectedness and taking responsibility for her arousal, Melissa was able to focus better on her husband's touch without her mind wandering. It also made their communication about sex more exciting because it was not just about frustration and disappointment.

The responsibility ticket can work the other way around too. Some partners feel that they must not be good-enough lovers because they can't seem to please their partners. Many women whose men have difficulty with their erections are convinced that they just aren't attractive enough. When they focus on this thought, they are unnecessarily taking on the responsibility for their partner's arousal.

This phenomenon is especially apparent in situations where men are focused on giving their woman an orgasm. Men derive much of their satisfaction in sex from knowing that they are good lovers (which is different from women, who primarily want to know that they are desirable[11]). Although there is something to be said for a lover who knows exactly how you like to be touched, the majority of women who have difficulty reaching orgasm are usually having difficulty with being disconnected or with relaxing sufficiently to really build a high level of eroticism and arousal. And it's not his responsibility, but hers to learn how to relax into her erotic thoughts and to communicate to her partner what she needs to build her arousal.

My office and email box are filled with complaints from people feeling as if they are "doing it" wrong because their partners don't experience pleasure, or from people who feel guilty about their fantasies or the things that arouse them. If you are thinking about sex this way, you are thinking backwards—believing that either you have responsibility for your partner's happiness or that they are responsible for yours. You are not accepting responsibility for your own sexual pleasure. Usually, people aren't very happy when I make this point because it goes against ideas heavily promoted in our culture about sexual arousal and turn-ons. The truth is that something can't be a turn-on for you unless your brain interprets it as a turn-on.

This doesn't mean you're not thinking about your partner's pleasure or trying to enhance it. Certainly, when your partner is aroused, your arousal gets boosted as well. Arousal builds on arousal, just as anxiety builds on anxiety, and detachment builds on detachment. But wanting your partner to have pleasure and enjoying them having pleasure are very different from feeling responsible for that pleasure. Likewise, if you wait for your partner to excite you, you are ignoring the fact that your thoughts affect the experience. You can just as easily orgasm from a slight touch (if you were that aroused) than you can from hours of stimulation. It's not common, but it's absolutely true.

The trouble is that people forget how to be aroused. The brain is programmed to pay less attention to things that it's already familiar with and more attention to things that are new. This means that it takes more effort to focus your attention on things that you know well, because your brain doesn't respond the same way as it does to something novel. It takes an effort to remind yourself of all of the things you find sexy and arousing about your partner after being with them for some time, because your brain doesn't pay as much attention as it did in the beginning.

Some people may interpret this as having lost interest in their partner, but that is a simplistic way of denying your responsibility to your sexual self. Other people continue to hold on to the idea that sex should be completely spontaneous at the same level of passion and excitement—even over time. That's just another way that they ignore how their brain actually works, and instead sets up unrealistic expectations for sex.

Good sex (for both partners) involves a balance between being connected to your partner and helping them enhance their own arousal while you focus on your own sexual ruthlessness. What this means is that in good sex, you are both attuned to what pleases your partner the most, and you are happy to give it, but you also are a little selfish in that you give yourself permission to think the most erotic thoughts and entertain the sexiest ideas and actions for yourself. Good sex in a long-term relationship requires that you keep a focus on those things about your partner that are the most attractive, the sexiest, and how much you enjoy them. Your mental focus will shape each individual experience as well as the character of your sexual relationship overall.

Taking responsibility for your sexual pleasure also means that your sexuality belongs to you and should not be ignored if you are alone or don't have a partner. How many people ignore their sexuality if they aren't in a relationship at the time? Your blood doesn't stop flowing, your hormones don't stop circulating through your body, your muscles are still working, and your brain is still fantasizing—unless you ignore your sexuality.

"Use it or lose it" applies to both your body and your mind, so it's just as important to continue to have sexual thoughts, sexual arousal, and sexual activity even if you are by yourself. If you ignore this, you are shunning your responsibility to your sexual self and letting that part of you get weaker and weaker—both physically and mentally.

If you don't have a current partner, masturbation is a common sexual practice that helps give sexual release and increase a sense of vitality and pleasure. Some people have very negative feelings or opinions about masturbation because of what they have been taught since childhood. Masturbation, however, is actually both quite natural and quite positive. It helps maintain the blood flow to your sexual organs and continues to reinforce in your brain your ability to experience sexual pleasure. Although porn can be an important source of erotic stimulation for both couples and individuals, learning how to masturbate without porn keeps your creative brain sharp and is yet another way you take responsibility for your sexual pleasure.

Learning to take back the reigns of your sex life is not always easy or straightforward. Women especially "receive" so many messages about how their partner will have some magical quality that will "do it" for them that it becomes hard to believe that all that power is really within yourself and how you think about things.

Here are some ways to start taking back your sexual power:

- Start to examine what sexual fantasies create the highest level of arousal in you rather than trying to suppress them.

- Tell your partner what you like physically and what pleases you in sex. If you haven't communicated that before, you can't assume that they automatically know. Nothing is obvious.

- Use masturbation to discover your own pleasure and power. This helps you explore your own particular sensations for the sake of pleasure. Although orgasm can be a big part of that experience, it shouldn't be the only focus.

- Understand that you turn yourself on or off by how you think about and judge things. Start to notice how you developed your particular ideas around sex.

- Develop a healthy sense of sexual selfishness by not feeling guilty over wanting to satisfy your desire. Remember that your partner wants you to experience *great sexual pleasure. You can focus on your own sexual pleasure while still being concerned for your partner's pleasure, and hopefully your partner will be doing the same!*

Chapter 5

Make Space for the Erotic

In order to have sexual pleasure in your life and in your experiences, you need to make room for it both in your physical world and your mental world. Either because of a lack of awareness or unrealistic expectations, many people believe that sex should "just happen" without any planning or preparation. This is one of the most common difficulties I see that people have when it come to their sex lives. The issue is that you need to make space in your life for sex to happen, both time-wise and thought-wise. You need to block out protected time for sex as well as create a protected mental space for sex and sexual thoughts. Without making space for sex and sexual pleasure both in your physical and mental life, you limit the amount of pleasure you can have. But when you make space for sex and the erotic, you invite more pleasure into your life.

It is a universal desire to want to get something without any effort, but it's foolish to expect it. A common wish is that sex will magically happen spontaneously without any planning—like a movie plot where two people see each other and just know. In real life, however, schedules get so complicated that there is usually no "extra" time or energy for sex to just happen. That's why making time and space for sex is so crucial.

Whenever I explain this to patients, I always remember a supervisor that I had in my residency who saw me seeing patient after patient most days without taking a lunch break.

When she asked me about it, I told her, "Sometimes people are late, and then other people come in without an appointment, so I don't really have time for lunch." She wisely told me that before I put any patients on my schedule, I should block out time for my lunch.

"That," she said "should be your protected time. You always need to protect some time for yourself." The wisdom of this is elegantly simple, but essential.

Making time is one way of making space for the erotic. You also benefit from thinking about those things that make sex more comfortable for you (peace and quiet in the house, the right temperature, a particular music track) and then planning to have those set in place. Little things like lube, a little towel, or a candle can make the difference between a smooth transition into sex, or scrambling to make it happen. Sometimes the best steps are the practical ones. Don't be afraid to tell your partner about some of these things either. Communicate with them about what time works best for both of you and what, if anything, you would like to do to prepare for sex. Making space for the erotic means not expecting your partner to read your mind or always be on the same page as you. Communication is crucial.

Do you need for sex to start earlier in the evening when you aren't so tired? Are you only comfortable with sex after both you and your partner have bathed? Can you only relax into sex when you know that the kids are asleep or can't hear you? There are some very concrete reasons why people find themselves having less sex than they would like. But there are also very practical solutions.

Planning doesn't guarantee good sex, or even sex at all, but it does increase the chance of it going your way. Do you need to feel freshly shaven? Do it. Would you like to be less tired to have sex? Consider if there are any days you could have sex in the morning or the afternoon. Each person has their set of circumstances that would improve sex, and each person needs to consider in what way they could make it better for themselves.

Making space for the erotic is also something that applies to your mental life as well. How you think about sex affects the way you experience sex and also communicates to others how you feel about it. Are you thinking about sex in a positive way that is erotic to you? Are you comfortable with your body and your sexual expression? Do you think about sex at all?

As people's lives become more complicated, they have less time to think about sex in a pleasurable and romantic way. But the more you think about sex ... the more you think about sex. That is the way the brain works, reinforcing what it practices. So are you giving yourself the opportunity to think about sex during the day? Are you allowing yourself pleasing thoughts and memories that would help reinforce positive feelings about sex?

Sometimes thoughts about sex become filled with anxiety. You may worry about your "performance," or worry that your partner may not like something about your body. Some people don't even realize that they have anxious thoughts because the worrying is so subtle. An example of this can be when a guy is thinking about how hard his erection is, or a woman is thinking about whether or not she is lubricated enough, or if you're going to be able to reach orgasm.

These are really worries that you won't be able to perform or participate somehow, which is not a very sexy thought at all. Since your brain can only think about one thing at a time, anytime you are wrapped up in an anxious thought, there is no space for sexy, erotic thoughts. It is pretty natural to have anxious thoughts, but what you do with them and how long you hold on to them in the moment ends up affecting your pleasure and your overall happiness.

If you pass over these thoughts and focus on the erotic instead, you will continue through arousal and make it easier to have pleasure and satisfaction. If you allow yourself to dwell on anxious thoughts, it usually starts a whole cascade of anxious feelings. This activates a stress response in your body that literally short-circuits sexual arousal.

It's pretty common for anxious thoughts to take over and leave no space for sexy thoughts. If you find this is happening to you, you can practice bringing your attention back to something you like about the present moment. Don't fight the anxious thought—just bring your attention back to your pleasure. Each time you practice doing this, the easier it becomes to do. By bringing your focus back to the erotic, you are doing a mental exercise that improves your ability to focus on what's erotic. The exercise described in Chapter 2 about focusing on a simple object in your hand for three minutes is very helpful in this situation as well. Making this space for the erotic is a very important way of increasing and enhancing your sexual pleasure.

Practice creating time and space, both mentally and physically, for the erotic. When you create space for sex to happen, you increase your chances for success. This is true for both the physical and the mental.

To enhance your eroticism and arousal, practice the following:

- *Be honest with yourself and your partner about what time of day works best for you to have sex.*

- *Block out days or times that are just for you and your partner to spend being sexual with each other (this doesn't have to be for intercourse).*

- *Make time each day, for just a few minutes, to have some pleasurable anticipation about sex or to have positive sexy thoughts.*

- *Notice if you have any anxious or negative thoughts during sex.*

- *Whenever you are having negative or anxious thoughts, take a deep, calming breath to activate your relaxation response.*

- *Instead of focusing on the negative or anxious thoughts, focus on some aspect of the pleasure you are experiencing at that moment—either something very pleasing about your partner or your own sensations.*

Chapter 6

Anger and Resentment

If you're going to be in a relationship with someone, inevitably there will be times when you get angry with your partner. It may be something they do or say (or something they don't do or say). But it really is unavoidable getting angry at some point. How you deal with that anger can significantly affect your sexual arousal and pleasure.

Remember Julie? When I asked her a little bit more about her husband helping her out with the boys, this is what she had to say.

"I think that dealing with the boys has really been the hardest part of our whole marriage. Don't get me wrong. I love them to death. But I just thought that I would like parenting more than I do. It's just awful having to do all the parenting stuff, and my husband doesn't seem to want to help me. It's like he assumes that I'm okay with doing everything because I'm the mom. I even get pretty angry at him when he's just sitting there watching TV, while I'm trying to cook and they're running around asking me for stuff. He'll help if I ask him to. I just wish he'd do it without me having to ask!"

It's clear that Julie was feeling angry about the disparity in their parenting responsibilities. What was more troubling was that it seemed that she was starting to resent her husband for it, which was seriously affecting their relationship.

ANGER

Anger is experienced on many different levels. At the physical level, anger activates your flight-or-fight response, which works directly against your sexual arousal response. On a psychological level, you may feel attacked, injured, unwanted, or dismissed as unimportant. Discussing your anger and finding common ground, a resolution, or forgiveness is essential to being completely open to sexual pleasure.

Different people have different levels of tolerance for being angry and sexually excited at the same time. This is why some people really enjoy makeup sex after an argument and may even create or exaggerate arguments so they can have makeup sex. For these people, makeup sex is part of their process of moving on. It is important to understand that not everyone likes makeup sex or having sex when they are still angry, and no one should insist that you have sex, or even *want* to have sex when you are still angry if that's not your style.

Regardless, if you don't deal with anger immediately, by discussing and resolving it with your partner, one way or another, it becomes deep-rooted as resentment. This resentment acts as a foundation on which future anger is laid, which then magnifies the anger and makes it feel out of proportion to the situation.

RESENTMENT

Resentment is much more insidious than anger. It happens when a person hangs on to anger in response to feeling wronged by someone else and is unable to let it go. Resentment causes the brain to relive the anger in ways that produce a negative emotional and physical reaction. It acts as an automatic trigger for anger that you feel you can't control. Resentment also creates distance between you and your partner because it focuses on the negative aspects of the situation that made you angry to begin with. Being resentful feels like you are a stick caught in the mud, unable to free yourself or move forward. And the longer you stay with resentment, the more your mental image of your partner will change for the worse. You actually end up focusing much more on the negative aspects of your partner, thereby enhancing your negative image of them.

Resentment keeps you feeling wronged—over and over again. It works against sexual arousal and pleasure because you are less likely to want to open yourself up to and share (physically or emotionally) with someone who you feel has hurt you. Resentment also takes much more effort to resolve than anger does. Many times it requires that you let go of being "right" and compromise about your differences. In order to overcome resentment after your partner has admitted a wrongdoing or a shortcoming, you need to make a concerted effort to try to understand the other person's point of view by putting yourself in their shoes. It's not an easy process, and it's one that many people struggle with in therapy.

The most important step in getting rid of resentment is practicing forgiveness. Forgiveness is for you. Forgiveness is *not* forgetting. Forgiveness doesn't mean you like or will accept a certain behavior. Forgiveness means that you will accept the other person and their attempts to move forward. Forgiveness is the part of your healing that allows you to let that person close to you again.

Without closeness, sex becomes very one-sided and one dimensional. When resentment exists within you, it prevents closeness and decreases your capacity for arousal and pleasure. Resentment is a trap that causes you to focus more on negative traits than positive ones. It may keep you feeling "right," but it also works to keep you feeling alone.

Just as anger can turn into resentment if not handled quickly, resentment can turn into contempt, which is even more toxic to the relationship. Contempt occurs when a person focuses so much on some negative aspect of a person that they start to view the other person as inferior to them. For example, a person might develop contempt for their partner after years of having them lie despite addressing it with the partner repeatedly. Contempt is a very bad sign for a relationship in general, and usually replaces sexual pleasure with disgust or repulsion. In fact, contempt has been found to be one of the most destructive forces in a relationship and a strong predictor of divorce.[12]

Luckily, Julie had not reached the point of contempt. She could easily identify many positive things about her husband and their relationship, and she could appreciate the times that he tried to help with the boys and around the house. And while a combination of factors contributed to Julie's decline in desire for sex with her husband, anger and resentment were keeping her stuck from addressing any of them.

Don't Delay in Dealing with Anger or Resentment

The most important thing to remember is to address anger soon after experiencing it. Don't pretend you don't feel it, and don't stuff it away for another time. Anger left to sit or ignored will eventually build into resentment, which could seriously threaten your sexual pleasure as well as your relationship overall. Since resentment develops over time with repeated episodes of anger, try to reconcile each argument or disagreement directly.

Here are some crucial points to remember when dealing with anger or resentment:

- *Address situations that make you angry soon after the experience instead of letting anger seethe inside you and possibly affect other things.*

- *Rather than accusing your partner of "always" or "never" doing something, just speak about one particular situation at a time and try to offer a suggestion about how you would have preferred it to go.*

- *Don't escalate the conversation by addressing more than one issue at a time or by bringing up the past.*

- *Address topics by how they make you feel rather than just criticizing your partner's behavior.*

- *Consider whether it is a particular detail that's making you angry or a deeper issue of the relationship that you need to address?*

- *Explore ways in which you might have contributed to the situation and made it more difficult for your partner rather than easier?*

Chapter 7

Physical Factors and Sexual Dysfunction

Going hand in hand with the idea that sex should always be spontaneous and effortless is the almost magical wish that sexual difficulties can be solved simply by fixing something physical. The notion that every problem has a quick fix is so seductive—especially if the fix comes in the form of an easy-to-take pill. Our culture certainly has pushed this message for quite some time, to the point where most of us feel that the solutions to our problems should be simple with fast results.

I wanted to first present many of the psychological barriers to good sex before having a discussion about some of the physical causes of sexual dysfunction, because I think that people underestimate the effect that their thinking and their mental patterns of anxiety or negativity have on their body and their sexual response. So often, patients will come into the office insisting that something is purely physical without considering how they may have gotten to that point.

Granted, I have found cases of women severely affected by their birth control or other medications that have resulted in pain with sex, or men with erectile dysfunction and/or difficulty reaching orgasm simply due to medication side effects. If found early enough, these issues can easily be reversed. But if sexual difficulties are present for a long time, it may take a while for the body to heal. In addition, a long-standing physical injury to the body not only creates physical symptoms, but also has an effect on the psychology of that person, as well as on their sexual relationship with their partner.

Just to point out how interconnected we all are, studies have shown that a man's sexual dysfunction can actually increase the incidence of sexual dysfunction in his female partner.[13] Obviously, his sexual difficulty will affect her psychological response to him. But because a person's psychological and physical aspects are constantly responding to each other, his physical functioning ends up affecting her physical functioning as well. This is because what happens in the mind and in interaction with others gets translated into the physical in the body. It's not surprising to hear this common aphorism of sex therapy—that a sexual dysfunction is not just one person's problem, but instead becomes the couple's problem.

This is precisely why, even though I always highlight the psychological factors at play in clients' sexual dysfunction, I am also attentive to resolving physical causes as soon as possible. I do want to point out, however, that there is a difference between physical symptoms and physical causes of sexual problems. The sexual difficulties that a person experiences may come in the form of a physical symptom, but the cause may not be immediately evident. A physical cause of a sexual difficulty, however, can be present for quite some time before an actual symptom develops. This can make it confusing for patients being confronted with a decision about making lifestyle changes.

For example, a man may have been smoking for twenty to thirty years before experiencing erectile dysfunction, so he may find it hard to accept that his smoking is the cause. Even though his body was able to handle that physical assault (which I consider cigarette smoking to be) at an earlier age and for a certain period of time, it doesn't mean that his body will be able to continue to compensate for it as he gets older. Once the damage reaches a certain level, he develops a symptom (in this case, his erectile dysfunction).

There is a lot of information here that I hope many of you will incorporate into your lives to *prevent* sexual dysfunction from happening. This means addressing some lifestyle issues even before getting a physical symptom. This is the best way to preserve good sexual functioning throughout your life. Even though it is more difficult to heal a physical problem than it is to prevent it, this doesn't mean that there aren't ways of reversing damage to the body. It takes acknowledging the problem first, taking responsibility for your sexual health, and then a committing to treating your body differently to optimize your sex life.

CONCEPTUALIZING THE PHYSICAL CAUSES OF SEXUAL DYSFUNCTION

How do I conceptualize the physical causes of sexual dysfunction? I like to break them down into four areas:

1. Messages from your body to your brain

2. How those messages are processed in the brain

3. Messages sent from the brain back to the body regarding arousal

4. Responsiveness of the body to those messages in the form of blood flow.

Even though the biology of all of these steps can get quite involved and are far too complex for our purposes here, I will break it down for you so that it makes practical sense. If we go back to Steve's case, we can better understand how someone's psychological workings can became manifest as physical issues, which then express themselves as sexual dysfunction (in Steve's case, erectile difficulties).

Messages from the Body to the Brain

Every physical touch and sensation is transmitted from the body to the brain via nerve endings. There are several things that enhance this process, and even more things that interfere with it. First of all, we know that testosterone has a role in the formation and maintenance of nerve cells. This is precisely why both men and women actually have a decrease in sensation from their genitals as they get older, because their testosterone levels drop with age.

There are several natural ways for both men and women to maintain optimal levels of testosterone for their age without resorting to taking testosterone supplements. The most effective ways are to get seven to eight hours of restful sleep and to decrease any sources of chronic stress. Insuring that your diet includes sufficient levels of zinc is necessary for testosterone production. Also, regular moderate exercise, including strength training, helps regulate levels of testosterone and decrease stress.

Of course, there are some cases in which testosterone replacement is strongly recommended. Examples of this are women who have had a surgical menopause, women who have very low functional levels of testosterone after being on birth control pills, and men with unusually low levels of testosterone after correcting any lifestyle factors that could be naturally lowering their testosterone.

Another cause of decreased sensation during sex is the physical manifestation of anxiety on the nervous system. In Steve's case, he was missing out on sensations because of anxiety. Although he was having stimulating physical contact, some of those messages weren't getting through to his brain. The interference was both psychological and physical. First, his brain was filtering out pleasurable messages in favor of focusing on anxiety. Next, he was holding quite a bit of tension in his body, both in his neck and shoulder area and in his lower back. The muscle tension related to his anxiety also made him less sensitive to physical touch.

Many people experience anxiety as a low-level muscle tension that shortens the length of the muscles, thereby increasing the chance for compression of nerves. As nerves get compressed, they cannot send messages from the body to the brain as efficiently, resulting in a decrease in sensations. If the effect is severe enough, a person may actually feel numb, and the brain will miss out on the pleasure of sexual stimulation. For Steve, decreasing muscle tension by stretching and decreasing his overall stress was crucial to regaining that sensation.

Stretching is an activity that is crucial to our body's health, but one that people often avoid, especially as they get older. If you've ever watched pets when they get up, you'll see just how routinely they stretch their entire body. In lieu of stretching, many people prefer to take anti-anxiety medications, which also act as muscle relaxants. Although this may be helpful in severe cases of muscle spasms, we will see how this affects the brain's ability to process the sensations coming from the body and actually increases sexual dysfunction.

Another cause of decreased transmission of signals from the body to the brain is diabetes and the way that it damages nerve tissues. Type 2 diabetes has been exponentially increasing over the last several decades and now has reached epidemic proportions. Current figures show that in the last thirty years there has been a 176 percent increase in the diagnosis of type 2 diabetes across all ages[14]. This diagnosis is made when the body can no longer properly control blood sugar after meals, and the blood sugar increases to levels where it starts to damage the tissues of the body. Nerve cells are particularly sensitive to increases in blood sugar, and diabetic neuropathy (destruction of the nerve cells) is a common result of poorly controlled diabetes. Diabetes is an extremely serious illness that damages multiple organs and tissues of the body, and irreversible sexual dysfunction is a very common symptom.

Another very difficult condition to deal with is pain that accompanies sex. Whenever there is a complaint of pain, a person should be tested for any infections first. Sexually transmitted infections (STIs) can easily be treated, but can cause significant damage if left untreated. Whenever an STI is diagnosed, there should be testing and treatment of the partner as well, to prevent a Ping-Pong effect of passing the infection back and forth between partners.

But STIs are not the only cause of sexual pain. In fact, either too much tension or too much weakness in the muscles of the pelvic floor can cause debilitating pain and even entrapment of nerves, making sex extremely uncomfortable, if not painfully impossible for either men or women. Some pain also seems to be related to overactivity of nerves. Although scientists still don't completely understand how this happens, some research points to a pattern of chronic inflammation in the body that triggers changes in the tissues and nerves. In fact, chronic inflammation may also be responsible for the development of such conditions as interstitial cystitis, endometriosis, and fibroids in women, or chronic nonbacterial prostatitis in men.

Most people are not aware that the standard American diet creates a great deal of inflammation and leads to things like leaky-gut, which wreaks havoc with the immune system and contributes to conditions like increased allergic reactions and autoimmune disorders, such as asthma, hypothyroidism, and psoriasis. It also fuels much of the chronic illness that is on the rise in our society, like arthritis, diabetes, and even cancer. Things like gluten, artificial preservatives, and sugar in your daily diet could be damaging not only your sex life in the long term, but your heart health, your risk for cancer, and your overall health as well.

In my approach to sexual pain, I urge patients to address the underlying causes of increased inflammation in their system while also using medications to improve their symptoms. This means taking gluten out of their diet, whether they have been found to be gluten sensitive or not. Not only does gluten directly cause leaky gut regardless of your immune sensitivity, but wheat and wheat products are broken down in your body so fast that they increase your blood sugar faster than a candy bar (even whole wheat)![15] Taking gluten out of your diet is a major lifestyle change that many people resist, until they start feeling better. For millions of people, removing gluten and sugar from their diets can mean the difference between preserving their sex life over their entire lifespan versus having increased sexual dysfunctions, even as early as in their twenties.

How the Brain Processes the Messages from the Body

In order for pleasurable sensations to create a sense of sexual arousal, those messages must be properly processed in your brain. This was a large part of what was making Steve have so much trouble getting and keeping his erection. Here's how it worked. We have already seen how Steve's brain was receiving considerably less information from his genitals and his body. But those messages that *were* getting through were being processed in a way that was working against his sexual arousal.

Instead of using any pleasurable sensations from his genitals to heighten his arousal, Steve used them to constantly analyze his performance. If he felt blood rushing into his penis to cause an erection, he would start thinking about how hard he was (or wasn't) and about how long he thought he would be able to keep his erection (or when he might lose it). Rather than being used to enjoying his sexual contact, his brain scrutinized every little detail of his erection. When this happens in the brain, the sensations are not passed along to increase sexual arousal, but instead contribute to a vicious cycle of anxiety.

Most of this book has focused on ways the brain psychologically processes information. But there are important physical factors that can affect how the brain processes information as well. One major player in this arena is alcohol.

In the United States, over 70 percent of people have used alcohol at one time or another, and over half of adults drink on a regular basis.[16] There are certainly great social pressures to drink, with the underlying message that you can't really enjoy yourself unless you are drinking. Besides insinuating that a person can't have a good time or be happy without alcohol, it promotes the idea that a good time is one where you can't remember what happened the night before. If you can't remember what happened, how do you know it was good?

Technically, that is called a blackout. The alcohol creates an amnesia that wipes your brain clean of memories for that period of time. But the most damaging effects, and what is more commonly responsible for decreasing sexual pleasure, is alcohol's toxicity. Alcohol actually slows down brain functioning in a dose-dependent way (the more alcohol you drink, the more your brain is slowed down and blunted).

Alcohol interferes with the workings of the brain so that it can't process information very well. One sign of this is when you start to have numbness in your face after too many drinks. I always remind people that if they can't feel their face too much, they probably can't feel their genitals much either. What you believe you can do, think, and feel while intoxicated is not what you actually can do, think, or feel.

At the most extreme end of the alcohol spectrum, after a certain level of intoxication, the brain slows down so much that it can no longer regulate your bodily functions and you stop breathing and die. Long before that point, however, your sex life suffers from an inability to process the sensations you may be having. Alcohol is also famous for decreasing the ability to get an erection, as well as delaying or interfering with reaching orgasm in both men and women.

There are several other substances that can interfere with the way that your brain processes the sensations it receives from the body. Painkillers and tranquilizers (anti-anxiety medications) are good examples of these. Illicit drugs, antidepressants, and medications for attention deficit disorder (ADD) or Parkinson's disease are other examples of drugs that can change the way the brain processes information and sometimes cause sexual side effects.

Hormones also have distinct effects on brain tissue and how the brain processes information. Although it is not known exactly how hormones affect sex drive, sexual desire, and sexual response, we know that there are many estrogen receptors in brain tissue. Testosterone also seems to play a very important role in sexual thoughts and motivation for sex. The more that is understood about how hormones affect sexual functioning at the level of the brain, the more it seems that both estrogen and testosterone work together to create both sexual desire and arousal.

I just want to point out that there is no exact correlation between testosterone levels and sexual desire, although there probably has to be a minimum level of both estrogen and testosterone present for desire and arousal to happen. Also, desire may be driven by the actual changes in hormone levels, which happens in normal cycles in the body, rather than just steady levels.

The Brain Communicating Messages Back to the Body

When the brain sends signals to the body, they travel along several different pathways—but they all go down the spinal cord. There are signals that belong to the fight-or-flight (stress) response, and there are signals that belong to the rest-and-digest response. Interestingly, the process of sexual arousal is controlled by the rest-and-digest response, despite the fact that we use the term "excitement" to describe it. Knowing this, it becomes easy to see how anxiety can short-circuit sexual arousal.

In Steve's case, this was exactly what was happening. When it came time for the brain to send messages back to the body related to what he was experiencing, most of the messages were those of stress. The fight-or-flight signals would surpass any signals of arousal, and his body was preparing for danger more than it was preparing for sex. Blood would be diverted away from the internal organs (including the genitals) so that it could be used by large muscle groups to either jump into action (fight) or run away (flight). Consequently, it was like shutting off the valve to his erection, and he would inevitably lose it.

Substances that increase anxiety, like large amounts of caffeine, can have the same effect on people, making it difficult to get erect, aroused, and/or lubricated. Some people are very sensitive to caffeine and don't realize that they may be getting multiple sources of caffeine in a day—in colas, tea, coffee, energy drinks, exercise supplements, diet pills, and even some painkillers like Excedrin, Midol Complete, and Panadol.

One very important factor that people don't often consider when thinking about sexual dysfunction is muscle tension causing chronic back problems. Since the nerves that are responsible for sexual response travel down the spine and branch out from between the vertebrae found in the lower back, problems with the lower back can also create difficulty for sexual functioning. Muscle tension interferes with both messages traveling from your body up to your brain as well as those on the way back from your brain to the body. Keeping the lower back strong and flexible is an important way to prevent damage to those nerves—and protect against osteoporosis too.

Most adults spend much of their days sitting at work or at home, which creates increased pressure on the vertebrae. Sitting for most of the day also causes the core muscles to become weak from lack of use. All of this adds up and causes compression fractures and herniated disks—just from sitting! So think about your sexual pleasure next time you have the choice to sit or stand.

How the Body Responds to Messages from the Brain to Increase Blood Flow

Finally, for good sexual response, there needs to be good blood flow. This happens when arteries receive the messages sent from the brain that tell them to relax and let more blood flow to the area.

Luckily, this is an area where Steve had no difficulties. In fact, once he practiced getting back in tune with the messages his body was receiving and was able to stop the anxious pattern of thinking with cognitive behavioral therapy in the office, his cycle of arousal could proceed naturally and his blood vessels responded beautifully. He reported that he was able to reliably get erections and was certainly feeling more pleasure overall.

When thinking about the responsiveness of blood vessels, many people will think of the hormone testosterone and the medication Viagra. It's true, hormones do play an important role in the ability of small arteries to widen and permit blood to fill the genital organs and erectile tissues. But it is estrogen specifically that has been found to assist in the vasodilation (opening up) of small arteries by several different mechanisms.[17] For example, estrogen helps increase levels of nitric oxide (NO), which is the same substance that Viagra increases to help with erections. For both men and women, estrogen is made from the conversion of testosterone, depending on what the body needs. Estrogen also decreases the effects of acute stress on blood vessels, keeping them from constricting too much.

One very important substance that needs mentioning is nicotine. Found in cigarettes, cigars, chewing tobacco, and electronic cigarettes, nicotine is one of the most potent vasoconstrictors (artery-closing substances) known to man. When a person takes a puff of a cigarette, for example, nicotine instantly courses through the bloodstream and starts to cause blood vessels to tighten up. This limits the amount of blood flow to the brain, to the heart, and—you guessed it—to the genitals. This means that even one cigarette can start to affect the amount of blood flow to the penis. Cigarettes have an immediate effect on genital blood flow as well as long-term damaging effects on the small arteries of the penis.[18] (By the way, nicotine gum has the same immediate effects on the small blood vessels, and some people actually chew more pieces of gum than they smoked cigarettes!)

Obviously, the body is an intricate system that not only tries to maintain a particular balance, but is also constantly responding to what we put in it. Even though the human body is capable of compensating for quite a bit of abuse, it's important to keep in mind that sexual dysfunction can be the result of so many things that we eat, drink, or otherwise consume, and some people are just much more sensitive than others. The trouble is you won't know if you are more sensitive until you have an actual problem.

How to protect your sexual functioning from physical factors:

- *Limit the amount of alcohol that you have at any one time—one drink or less is optimal.*

- *Consider eliminating all wheat products and other gluten-containing grains from your diet*

- *Cut back on sweets and added sugar. Try not to use artificial sweeteners instead of sugar, since many of these create toxic chemicals in your body.*

- *Exercise regularly. This helps balance your hormones naturally, as well as increases good blood flow to all of your tissues, especially your genitals.*

- *Have regular sexual activity, at least two to three times per week. If you don't have a sexual partner, masturbation should be an important part of your routine. Use it or lose it.*

- *Make sure that you get at least seven to eight hours of sleep every night and take zinc and selenium*

supplements   regularly—these   are   necessary   for
testosterone production for both men and women.

- *Find ways to reduce chronic stress in your everyday life. Stress lowers your testosterone levels over time and continuously activates your stress response.*

Conclusion

Imagine that your sexual self had a voice. What would it say to you? How often would you sit down and converse with your sexual self, catching up with how it's doing and asking if it's happy? Would you ask it things like "How's life been treating you lately?" or "Where do you see yourself five years from now?"

How does your sexual self try to communicate with you now? Are you tuned into the messages it's trying to send you, or does it seem like a distant voice difficult to understand? Have you given your sexual self permission to express itself and continue to evolve throughout your life? Do you celebrate it and throw it a party every once in awhile?

Your sexual self is intrinsically connected to every other aspect of your being. This is why sexual desire and expression can be so strongly impacted by our internal thoughts and feelings and by how you are treated when interacting with others. The reality is that you have a responsibility to your sexual self, just as you have to the rest of yourself—by maintaining a healthy weight and a healthy heart, getting enough mental stimulation, keeping your hormones balanced, or by striving for spiritual joy and peace.

Your body and mind communicate constantly with one another to create the reality of each moment, and there is a mutual and continuous response between them to what is happening internally and externally. Being able to hear and understand that communication fosters the growth and happiness of your sexual self and every other dimension of who you are.

I hope that this book has been a way to start looking at the different ways that your sexual self is silenced (through disconnection), misled (through unrealistic expectations), enslaved (by giving your power away), ignored (by not giving it time and attention), or held hostage (by anger and resentment).

Although the physical aspects of sex must be addressed whenever there is pain or discomfort, they are simply the tip of the iceberg when it comes to your sexual functioning and happiness. Desire is driven by many variables, including hormones, energy level, self-esteem, guilt, obligations, and how you feel about your partner to name a few.

When it comes to sexual desire and pleasure, your complexity as a human being is both your biggest blessing and your greatest obstacle. So much of your sexual pleasure and satisfaction is determined by internal factors that seem isolated from sex—but really aren't.

For Julie, there were many different layers to her lack of sexual desire. All of these layers were blocked by the anger and resentment she had toward her husband as well as toward her role in being a mother. Once we worked through the layers, with the help of her husband, she started to give her sexual self permission to explore what was most erotic for her—being so desirable that a man would overcome any obstacle to be with her—a notion she was trying very hard to repress because she thought it was so unacceptable.

There was also a physical obstacle to her enjoying sex with her husband. Her lack of available testosterone as a result of changes from taking birth control pills was making sex somewhat painful, even though she hadn't mentioned this initially and revealed it only after I took a detailed history pertaining to her sexual activity. In exploring this, she came to understand that her lack of sexual desire was not because of wanting to avoid sex with her husband, but instead was about wanting to avoid the physical pain that came along with it. That pain, layered with her anger and resentment on top, created a wall that kept her from enjoying sex with him and had her doubting the health of her sexual self.

Melissa's case was a little different. She was not having pain and did not require any physical treatment. Instead, she learned that her distraction was pulling her away from the pleasure and excitement of sex with her partner, and she was having difficulty just being fully present there with him.

Although she was making time for sex with her husband, she was not making mental space for the erotic within her.

For Melissa, some exercises around mindfulness and attention when it came to sexual pleasure helped her get reconnected to the experience of sensuality. She also found that she could more easily switch from mommy-mode to sexy woman-mode when she worked on how the identity of her sexual self had been swallowed up by all of her other responsibilities.

Good sex is about relaxing into pleasurable physical and emotional messages constantly being sent back and forth between your body and your brain. Fostering the best environment for your sexual self will give you the opportunity for the greatest success and pleasure in your sex life. Even if all seems lost, you can find your way back to your sexual self and create the best environment for it to grow and flourish for your entire life.

Acknowledgments

Although the majority of this book comes from the common themes that I repeatedly discuss with patients in my practice, the book itself would never have manifested without the countless hours of writing and rewriting my thoughts. My thanks and love to Ken for his patience throughout the entire process. Next, I would like to thank all of my "Sisters" in supporting and encouraging me – you know who you are. A special thanks to Vincent for his words of advice and example. Thank you to my editor, Candace Johnson for such helpful suggestions and detailed work. Thanks also to Suzy for her spunk and inspiration. And a special thank you to Melanie who guided me toward the discipline I needed to get this done.

Notes

Chapter 1: How to Conceptualize Sexual Difficulties

1. West, S. L., D'Aloisio, A. A., Agans, R. P., Kalsbeek, W. D., Borisov, N. N., and Thorp, J. M. 2006. "Prevalence of low sexual desire and hypoactive sexual desire disorder in a nationally representative sample of US women." *Archives of Internal Medicine* 168(13):1441–1449.

2. Nicolosi, A., Laumann, E. O., Glasser, D. B., Moreira Jr, E. D. Paik, A., and Gingell, C. 2004. "Sexual behavior and sexual dysfunctions after age 40: The global study of sexual attitudes and behaviors," *Urology* 64(5):991–997.

3. Reiche, E. M., Odebrecht Vargas Nunes, S., and Kaminami Morimoto, H. 2004. "Stress, depression, the immune system, and cancer." *The Lancet Oncology* 5(10):617–625.

4. Kubzansky L. D. and Thurston, R. C. 2007. "Emotional vitality and incident coronary heart disease: Benefits of healthy psychological functioning." *Archives of General Psychiatry* 64(12):1393–1401.

5. Carmody, J., Reed, G., Kristeller, J., and Merriam, P. 2008. "Mindfulness, spirituality, and health-related symptoms." *Journal of Psychosomatic Research* 64(4):393–403.

Chapter 2: How Disconnection and Dissociation Affect Sex and Desire

6. Basson, R. 2005. "Women's sexual dysfunction: revised and expanded definitions." *Canadian Medical Association Journal* 172(10):1327–1333.

7. Amen, Daniel. 2013. *Unleash the Power of the Female Brain.* New York: Harmony Books, p. 36.

Chapter 3: Expectations and Sexual Pleasure

8. Elsenbruch, S., Schmid, J., Bäsler, M., Cesko, E., Schedlowski, M., and Benson, S. 2012. "How positive and negative expectations shape the experience of visceral pain: an experimental pilot study in healthy women." *Neurogastroenterology & Motility* 24(10): 914–922.

9. Plassman, H., O'Doherty, J., Shiv, B., and Rangel, A. 2008. "Marketing actions can modulate neural representations of experienced pleasantness." *Proceedings of the National Academy of Science* 105(3):1050–1054

10. Lambert, N. M., et al. 2011. "Expressing gratitude to a partner leads to more relationship maintenance behavior." *Emotion* 11(1):52–60.

Chapter 4: You Are Responsible for Your Sexual Arousal

11. Bergner, D. 2013. *What do women want?* (Edinburgh: Canongate), p. 75.

Chapter 5: Make Space For the Erotic

None

Chapter 6: Anger and Resentment

12. Gottman, J. M. 2014. *What predicts divorce: The relationship between marital processes and marital outcomes* (New York: Psychology Press), p. 24.

Chapter 7: Physical Factors and Sexual Dysfunction

13. Shindel, A., Quayle, S., Yan, Y., Husain, A. and Naughton, C. 2005. "Sexual dysfunction in female partners of men who have undergone radical prostatectomy correlates with sexual

dysfunction of the male partner." *Journal of Sexual Medicine* 2(6): 833–841.

14. http://www.cdc.gov/diabetes/statistics/prev/national/figage.ht m

15. Davis, W. 2011. *Wheat belly: Lose the wheat, lose the weight, and find your path back to health* (New York: Rodale), p. 35.

16. http://www.cdc.gov/nchs/data/series/sr_10/sr10_260.pdf

17. Tostes, R. C., Nigro, D., Fortes, Z. B., and Carvalho, M. H. C. 2003. "Effects of estrogen on the vascular system." *Brazilian Journal of Medical and Biological Research* 36(9):1143–1158.

18. Ledda, A., Belcaro, G., and Laurora, G. 1996. "Vasculogenic erectile dysfunction: Diagnosis," in *Vascular Andrology*, ed. Andrea Ledda (Berlin: Springer), p. 8.

About the Author

Madeleine M. Castellanos, MD, is a practicing psychiatrist who specializes in sex therapy, hormone supplementation, and functional medicine consulting. She is a member of the American Association of Sexuality Educators, Counselors and Therapists (AASECT), the Society for Sex Treatment and Research (SSTAR), the International Society for the Study of Women's Sexual Health (ISSWSH), the International Society for Sexual Medicine (ISSM), the North American Menopause Society (NAMS), the American Psychiatric Association (APA), and the Institute for Functional Medicine (IFM). Driven by her passion for teaching others about the connection between body and mind, both in sex and in overall health, she lectures, holds workshops, speaks with the media, and sees private patients. She lives in New York City.

You can find more information on her website at www.TheSexMD.com. Or visit her on Facebook (The Sex MD), at Twitter (@DrCastellanos), at Google+ (The Sex MD), or on Instagram (thesexmd).

CPSIA information can be obtained
at www.ICGtesting.com
Printed in the USA
FFHW01n0247270718
47563322-51037FF